I'm Thinking *of* Leaving My Husband

by
Rebekah Prewitt

LakeCityCounsel.com

Dedication

To the daughters of Sara

Table of Contents

Introduction

*Come unto me, all ye that labour and are heavy laden, and I will give
you rest. Take my yoke upon you, and learn of me; for I am meek and
lowly in heart: and ye shall find rest unto your souls.
For my yoke is easy, and my burden is light.*
—*Matthew 11:28-30*

*A*re you unhappy in your marriage? Are you
thinking of moving on with your life?
Perhaps you have moved out, but you are not sure if
you've done the right thing. Before you go forward,
you might find this book helpful.

Many times, especially if the wife comes from a
religious background, she feels guilty for leaving her
marriage, but suppose she has legitimate grounds to
leave and doesn't know it. What if she does not have
grounds to leave? How does she live in a difficult
marriage? With the help of the Lord, *I'm Thinking of
Leaving My Husband* will help wives sort through the

fog of confusion in their struggle for direction and peace on this issue.

It is certainly no secret that many wives feel torn in their marriage. They may want a happy life with their spouse, but the deep wounds prevent this reality. Maybe their husband committed adultery and they are not sure how to continue with him after a blow like this. Perhaps the husband has a life controlling addiction like pornography or alcoholism, and he is destroying the whole family. Maybe the situation is not as extreme but the husband and wife have just slowly drifted apart in their marriage. The intimacy and feelings of affection are simply not there anymore. What should the wife do?

Fanny's Story

Is it okay to leave your marriage if you and your spouse have grown apart? Surprisingly, such was the case with the famous Christian hymn writer, Fanny Crosby. Fanny Crosby was blind, but in-spite of this handicap, she penned thousands of songs that are still in our church hymnals today. Songs like, "To God Be the Glory," "Blessed Assurance," "Tell Me the Story of Jesus," and "Praise Him! Praise Him!" It is said that she wrote so many hymns that she had to go by other names so as to disguise her songs, yet in spite of writing such rich God honoring songs, Fanny Crosby, was among those whose marriage ended because she and her husband drifted apart.

The story goes that at the age of thirty-five, Fanny was still a single woman. At that time, she fell in love with Van Alstyne. Van was a musician and, interestingly enough, was also blind. Van and Fanny were both interested in poetry and music which naturally drew them closer to each other. They married and moved from Manhattan to the little town of Maspeth, New York. From this union was birthed one child that died in infancy. Fanny had enjoyed her quiet life with Van in the small town, but after the death of her baby, she soon wanted to be back in the hustle and bustle of things. So, the Alstynes moved back to Manhattan.

This move however, proved to be disastrous for their marriage because they started to drift apart from each other. They each had their own group of friends and apparently resigned themselves to being just friends instead of husband and wife. Sadly, their twenty-something years of marriage ended. Fanny spent the last quarter of her life as a single woman while still writing hymns and being deeply involved in mission work.

Did Fanny really do the wrong thing in allowing her marriage to end? You might be surprised at the answer.

In the next chapter, I will outline two major grounds by which a wife can Biblically leave her husband. Do either of these or both apply to you? Let's find out.

Chapter 1

Grounds for Divorce

Ground #1 – Fornication

And I say unto you, Whosoever shall put away his wife, except it be for fornication, and shall marry another, committeth adultery: and whoso marrieth her which is put away doth commit adultery.
—*Matthew 19:9*

*H*as your husband committed fornication? Fornication simply means illicit or unlawful sexual intercourse. Jesus said in Matthew 19:9, "And I say unto you, Whosoever shall put away his wife, except it be for fornication, and shall marry another, committeth adultery: and whoso marrieth her which is put away doth commit adultery."

Are you leaving your husband because he committed fornication? You may have noticed that Jesus used the term "fornication" in His exception clause. Why did He do this? I have learned that fornication covers a wide variety of sexual sins. While for one wife it may be that her husband had sex with her best friend, for another, it could mean that her husband had sex with animals or sex with a man. For this reason, Jesus wanted to provide a wide exception when He used the term fornication. Isn't He a kind God. If Jesus had used the word adultery here, He would have limited the exception. By using the term fornication, Jesus provided grounds for the dissolution of marriage if your husband has sex with anyone else but you.

The God-Given Escape

If this is you, you are Biblically qualified to leave and remarry, and it will not be counted against you as an adultery. Some may have a hard time with this especially if they were taught all their life that God hates divorce. May I remind you, however, of the fact that God Himself wrote a bill of divorcement and gave it to Israel because they committed adultery against Him. Are you better than God? Jeremiah 3:8 says, "And I saw, when for all the causes whereby backsliding Israel committed adultery <u>I had put her away, and given her a bill of divorce</u>." If you are feeling guilty, don't operate on your feelings. I have learned that when God provides an escape out of a situation, **take it** (1 Corinthians 10:13).

I have seen wives who don't take the escape. Instead, they try to remain in their marriage with a husband who has well and soiled himself in deep sexual sin. They try to stick it out hoping and praying that things will get better. Often, however, they are left battling the heart wrenching emotions of those scars. These wives are constantly watching their husbands asking detailed questions about the affair—time and place and how and what. These are details that the enemy uses against the wife day after day. He plagues her mind as he rehearses the scenes before her eyes thus breaking her down even further.

The wife who remains in the marriage after an adultery suffers with feelings of insecurity. She may see herself as unattractive and seek to improve her appearance. She may question, *What is wrong with me? Why am I not good enough?* She may even begin to feel that this was her fault. Maybe if she had done this or that, then perhaps this would have never happened. Plus, the wife who stays may spend years having her husband grovel at her feet trying to make up for what he has done to her. She may want him and others to feel sorry for her, seeking pity. Sometimes, she will seek revenge because she wants him to know what it feels like if it was the other way around. Remaining in the marriage after her husband commits fornication also puts the wife in a position to exert the upper hand. Obviously in her mind her husband is not fit or not capable of making good decisions anymore; therefore, she will have to do it. Furthermore, many times, the wife who stays can be viewed as the hero or the stronger one receiving praise for her noble act by well meaning friends and family members. Yet, this is an unhealthy attitude for her to assume.

As you can see, there are many issues to work out when the wife decides to stay in the marriage. Now, I am not saying that the Bible requires a wife to leave in such circumstances, but I am saying that it is good to take the escape when we are provided with one. It may make for a happier life for you. Trying to be strong and tough it out may not be the wisest of decisions.

We don't always know what is best for us, but God does. He did provide this escape. It is not at all a poor reflection on the wife if she chooses to take it. Sadly, however, many times a wife will make up her mind to do things her own way thinking that she is doing the right thing. In reality, however, the opposite is true. Maybe she hopes to please a pastor, or parent, or even her husband instead of listening to the voice of God on the matter. Unfortunately, she will likely reap the consequences of that decision.

A Criminal Offense

The wife who has experienced the blow of adultery may not realize it, but a serious crime was committed against her. I think of this like when a crime is done in society. For instance, have you ever had your home broken into, or perhaps had something like a car stolen? If not, think of some crime that you ever had to deal with. How did it make you feel? Did you feel violated? That's how I feel when I encounter a crime scene. I feel violated. An injustice has just taken place. Even if it was not done to me personally, there is still an air that something bad has just happened. It is a sobering experience that heightens my awareness to the evil that surrounds me. Similarly, when it comes to the matter of adultery, the Bible refers to it as a heinous crime (see Job 31:11). When a woman discovers that her husband has committed adultery, there is a crime that has just been brought to light. With that discovery, she immediately feels the shaking and trauma of that transgression. Fornication is a crime against God and against those who have been the victims of it. If this is you my dear wife, you have had a grave crime committed against you. Understanding it to be so will be important for your healing process. You will not make good decisions nor heal properly if you do not understand that your husband is a criminal in this regard.

Ground #2 – Forsaken

Let's assume for a moment that you are a Christian wife whose husband has simply walked away. Possibly your husband even claims to be a Christian. Is it okay for a wife to move on with her life if her husband leaves?

Some years ago, my husband and I learned from a friend that her husband left her. She didn't really know why he left. He only told her that he wanted out of the marriage. Then, he packed his bags and was gone. When I first learned of this tragedy in her life, I have to admit, I encouraged her to hold on because I thought maybe her husband would come back home again. I later learned that this kind of advice is not Biblical. Yes, in one sense, love is patient; however, in another sense, God allowed for this wife to have an escape out of her marriage. Here is the escape clause:

1 Corinthians 7:15

The Apostle Paul writes, "But if the unbelieving depart, let him depart. A brother or a sister is not under bondage in such cases: but God hath called us to peace."

Did you see that? "A brother or a sister is not under bondage." If your husband left you, then this verse applies to you. You are not in bondage to the law of marriage any longer. Why? Because, "God hath called us to peace." Maybe you have pleaded and prayed for your husband to come back, yet he does not want to. The Bible says to let him go. Don't fight him to come back. Yes, this may be difficult to do. After all, this is the man you hoped to spend the rest of your life with. He may be the father of your children and the man you love dearly. However difficult it may seem to do, God will not tell you to do something that He cannot supply the strength by which you can do it. In fact, the Lord is quite familiar with what you are experiencing, for He Himself was forsaken. He has been forsaken many times.

The prophet Jeremiah tells us that "Surely *as* a wife treacherously departeth from her husband, so have ye dealt treacherously with me, O house of Israel, saith the LORD" (Jeremiah 3:20). Did you notice that God considers what your husband has done to be treachery? Treachery is closely akin to treason which historically has been a capital offense. Like in the last section, you must learn to recognize your husband as a criminal in the eyes of God. This will be very important for your healing.

In the book of Judges, we see another example of how the Children of Israel forsook the Lord.

> And the children of Israel cried unto the LORD, saying, We have sinned against thee, both because we have forsaken our God, and also served Baalim. And the LORD said unto the children of Israel, Did

not I deliver you from the Egyptians, and from the Amorites, from the children of Ammon, and from the Philistines? The Zidonians also, and the Amalekites, and the Maonites, did oppress you; and ye cried to me, and I delivered you out of their hand. Yet ye have forsaken me, and served other gods: wherefore I will deliver you no more. Go and cry unto the gods which ye have chosen; let them deliver you in the time of your tribulation (Judges 10:10-14).

As you can see, God was quite angry with the children of Israel, and He had every right to be. After they forsook Him, He also forsook them.

Friend, under these circumstances if you are feeling guilty for ending your marriage, please don't. Your husband is the one who has physically forsaken you. This applies to whether your husband claims to be a Christian or not. You are free to leave the marriage. There is no reason for you to sit around waiting for years hoping that he will come back. Let me add here that if your husband has been married to someone else and then tries to return to you, there is an Old Testament principle that teaches that you are not to be with him again anyway. That would be an abomination before the Lord (see Deuteronomy 24:1-4). You need to move forward with your life in Christ without him.

It is important to understand that if your "Christian" husband (and I use that term loosely) has walked away from the marriage, he has also walked away from his Christian responsibility and is walking in disobedience to God. He is in essence saying, *I don't have respect for God nor His word any longer. I am going to do life my way.* When a "Christian" spouse departs from doing what is right, they are living in sin and have chosen that sin over both God and their family. According to the Bible, the person who leaves is operating as an unbeliever and no longer as a Christian. May I put you in remembrance of this verse? "But if the **unbelieving** depart, let him depart. A brother or a sister is not under bondage in such *cases:* but God hath called us to peace" (1 Corinthians 7:15).

Furthermore, the Apostle Paul made the following statement: "Art thou bound unto a wife? seek not to be loosed. Art thou loosed from a wife? seek not a wife" (1 Corinthians 7:27). You, dear wife have been loosed from your marriage. Did you know that the term "forsaken" meant loosen in Hebrew. We know that the Apostle Paul was steeped in the Law (Old Testament), so I find it very interesting that he would use the term "loosed" here (which means loosen or break up, dissolve, destroy, put off) as it relates to a husband and wife.

Wife, the Lord knows what has happened to you, and He knows what it feels like to be refused. He, unlike your husband, is not finished with you. He said, "For the LORD hath called thee as a woman forsaken and grieved in spirit, and a wife of youth, when thou wast refused, saith thy God" (Isaiah 54:6).

Many times wives feel guilty to leave a marriage because they have heard that God hates divorce, so they try to stick it out. Yet, God has allowed for divorce on certain grounds (See "Broken by Divorce" tract in the back of this book). You see, it really does not matter who files the paperwork, but rather who broke the covenant. Are you leaving your marriage because your husband forsook you?

In summary, if you are leaving your marriage because of either fornication or being forsaken, then these are the two Biblical grounds by which you can be free from your marriage. Are you leaving your husband for either of these two reasons? If so, then you are perfectly justified before God to do so. Go ahead and do what God has said in His Word that you can do.

Chapter 2

My Husband is an Addict

*A*fter reading Chapter 1, you might say, *I don't have Biblical grounds for leaving my husband, but how do I live with a husband who is addicted to _____.*

Pornography

Pornography is a major problem in homes, and many wives are devastated to say the least when faced with this sin in their husbands' lives. Does pornography, however, fall under the category of fornication? In other words, can a wife leave her husband if he is involved with pornography? After all, Jesus did say in Matthew 5:28, "But I say unto you, That whosoever looketh on a woman to lust after her hath committed adultery with her already in his heart."

One thing I would like to point out from Matthew 5:28 is the term "heart." It is in his heart and not in his body that he has sinned. Do you remember what the Apostle Paul said to the Corinthians? "What? know ye not that he which is joined to an harlot is one body? for two, saith he, shall be one flesh . . . Flee fornication. Every sin that a man doeth is without the body; but he that committeth fornication sinneth against his own body" (1 Corinthians 6:16,18). We have here further clarification on the term "fornication." Fornication is a sin against a man's own physical body. If there is no sexual intercourse, then it isn't fornication. Pornography, even though a sin, does not physically involve a sexual act with another person. The sin is through the eyes and in the heart rather than in the body. If you remember, the woman that they threw before Jesus was caught in the "very act" of adultery (John 8:4). Biblically speaking, pornography would be seen as adultery in the heart rather than fornication in the body; therefore, it does not constitute grounds for a wife to leave her husband. So, how does a wife live with a husband that is addicted to pornography? Keep reading.

Alcohol/Substance Abuse

What if a wife has an alcoholic husband? This is a common question. Wives are in a terrible predicament when their husbands are alcoholics. This life dominating sin in a husband affects the whole family. The wife is not being cared for like she should be, and the children suffer because of their father's stronghold. A wife may find that she is always picking up after her drunken husband and making excuses for him. Sometimes she goes without money. Other times, she experiences physical, emotional, and verbal abuse. Not to mention, the wife is often left to playing both parental roles in the home.

How does a wife cope with all of this stress? The simplest solution that the wife may conclude is to leave the marriage and do what is best for her and her children. With that said, however, if the wife is a Christian, she might wrestle with the decision to leave. How does a wife cope with an alcoholic husband? Does God really want her to stay in an awful marriage? Before I answer these questions and talk about how to live in a difficult marriage, let me shed some light on the foundational principles that a wife needs to understand before she can strive for peace and direction on this issue.

Foundational Principles

The Lord has ordained it so that a wife should be under the protection and care or her husband. At one time, the woman lived under the care and protection of her father, and then at her marriage, she was transferred to her husband's care. Once a wife comes under her husband's headship, it is there that she is placed. F. B. Meyers points out,

> It is very interesting to notice that while the Gospel so clearly insists on the divine order, it has elevated woman to be man's true helpmeet, and has caused her to be honored and loved as the glory of man. Neither society, nor family life, nor woman herself, can be happy unless she attains her true position.[1]

When a wife wrongfully steps aside from the marriage because of some problem in the home, she is left exposed to any and every danger that Satan can hurl at her. Whatever elements of life fall on her, she will not be protected from them any longer. It is like an umbrella on a rainy day. If you step outside of the umbrella, you are going to get wet. For this reason, the wife must understand where she belongs. I am reminded of an insightful statement I once heard by a certain wife. She said, "I would rather stand under the umbrella, even if it had holes, than to be outside of the will of God." She was right. I realize you might be frustrated because you are not seeing any hope for your marriage, but there is a God who specializes in the hopeless. He said, "Behold, I am the LORD, the God of all flesh: is there any thing too hard for me? (Jeremiah 32:27).

The Will of God

What does God want the wife to do? This is where the will of God comes into the question. If the wife does not have Biblical grounds to leave, then there remains only one option—she must stay with her husband. If she has already left, she must return. This is what the Lord thinks is best for her. He told us in 1 Corinthians 7:10, "And unto the married I command, yet not I, but the Lord, Let not the wife depart from her husband." You see, there are times in our lives when we feel like we must make a decision on a certain issue, but in reality, some decisions the Lord has already made for us. All we have to do is follow His directions as we see here in 1 Corinthians 7:10.

One of the reasons wives struggle for peace and direction as to what to do is because they are not only wrestling with their own will but also the will of their Creator. That is why there is such turmoil inside of the wife when she leaves. The will of God says, "Stay." Her will says, "Go." Who is going win? Many times the wife's will wins, but is there ever any real winning when you disobey the Lord? The Lord will allow people to go their own way. He may protest, but ultimately He will let the person decide. If, however, the wife makes the decision to be reconciled to her husband, she will immediately find clarity of thought. Her spiritual man will be at peace because she is not wrestling with God any longer on the issue, and she will have direction for her life once again. Until that time, the wife will be in limbo.

Chapter 3

Limbo and the Lure

*L*imbo is a horrible place to be. While you are there, you will find it hard to make concrete decisions for your future. It is a state of confusion, but God is not the author of confusion. You see, one of the devil's ploys is to draw the wife out from under the protection of God, and if he can draw her out, then he can do her in.

Do you remember the matter of Baalpeor? The prophet Balaam was hired to curse the children of Israel, but he could not do it because God's hand of protection was upon them. So, after several failed attempts, Balaam counseled the Moabites to commit whoredom with the children of Israel. Once they were lured out from under the "umbrella" of God's protection, the Lord sent a plagued upon them (Numbers chapters 23-31). And guess what, they were cursed. This time not by the enemy, but by God Himself.

A few years ago, I was talking to a young man over the phone who was feeling quite distressed and uneasy in his house. He said to me that he and his girlfriend were seeing spirits in the house. Fortunately, I had just read a verse in the Bible earlier that day which gave me the answer as to why this young man was so troubled. The verse actually took me by surprise because when we think of being cursed, who do we naturally think of? The devil. But in this verse I saw it differently. Proverbs 3:33 states, "The curse of the LORD is in the house of the wicked." You see, if you're going to live in fornication, God is going to curse your house. Similarly, when a wife is allured out from her home, she is going to have trouble.

Other Men

Just as Balaam counseled the Moabites to commit fornication with the children of Israel in hopes of seeing them cursed, the devil will use certain men in your life to lure you out of your marriage. It might be a coworker, a guy at the grocery store, a neighbor, or even a man at your church. Regardless of the man, the devil will use men who are his servants to draw you out from under the protection of God. Take for instance, Jackie.

> Jackie and her husband, Jeff, recently joined a new church and befriended Luis and Marissa. They were a friendly couple, so they all started hanging out together, but something alarming was happening inside of Jackie. She suddenly felt an attraction towards Luis. When Luis was around, she felt nervous. She also started having weird thoughts of running away with him. Her thoughts of Luis were so pronounced that Jackie felt like she was having a major problem.

> One day, Jackie's husband, Jeff, shared some news with her about Luis that gave her peace of mind. Jeff had been talking to Luis, when Luis blurted out that he had run away with his boss's wife, Marissa. All of a sudden, unknown to Jeff, Jackie felt confirmation that what she was

experiencing had nothing to do with her at all. Rather, the Lord may have been revealing to her that Luis was not a holy man.

Dear wife, if you suddenly notice that you feel uncomfortable and nervous around a certain man, it may be that the Lord is trying to give you a warning. Often, if there is a man who is struggling with lust, you may think that you are falling for him when in reality he is the one who has the problem. All these things are baits of Satan that he sets up hoping to lure you away from your marriage. If you act upon those feelings, you have played into his hand. If, however, you recognize that God may be allowing you to feel funny around a certain man so that you can keep your distance, then the devil has lost.

Also, if you find that you are having private thoughts of being with other men, don't allow yourself to enjoy them or muse on them. Don't do this even if it is just for a little moment. Immediately reject those thoughts. Don't let your heart be carried away into any evil, and don't give the devil even a little pinch of pleasure in the forbidden. Let your breastplate of righteousness be strong as iron, and let your helmet of salvation cover your head. Don't let your mind feast on wickedness—not even for one minute. In fact, one minute is way too long. It could be that the man who comes to your mind is an unchaste man, or it could be that you are being drawn away by your own lusts. This is why Christian women should live spiritually sober lives everyday. If you don't, you might mistakenly interpret what you are feeling and plunge headlong into misery. Some of you may have heard of Phil Driscoll, the trumpet player. He sang a song that said, "Don't dance with the devil, he will make a fool out of you." This will happen one hundred percent of the time if you take Satan's bait in any form it comes.

Wife, I encourage you not to play with those lustful, flirty, jokey, flattering spirits. You won't have power to overcome the devil if you play with him. Men who tell lots of jokes and keep you smiling—pay attention to that kind. Avoid laughing with them. Also avoid men who are complementary, flirty, say offhanded statements, or make comments with sexual innuendos. Confront them if need be. Remember, the devil always paints the grass greener on the other side. Similarly, if you have to work in an environment with men, avoid going on business trips alone with them. Don't go out for lunch with them, and as much as possible, avoid being alone with a man—period. If you have to talk to a man on the phone for some reason, keep your conversation brief. If you find that you have a certain man that is luring you over the phone, let your husband start handling that business with him.

In addition, don't keep secrets from your husband about other men. The devil is crafty, and he likes to operate in darkness and secrecy. As soon as you notice that there is something funny about the way you feel with a certain man, reveal it to your husband. Eventually, the two of you will get comfortable with learning how to fight this spiritual battle that all you will have to say is, "Honey, you deal with this guy. He makes me feel a little funny." By that time, your husband will have had enough experience with you to know what you are dealing with and that the problem is not you. So, don't keep secrets from your husband about other men. Expose them. When you do, you are also exposing the traps of the enemy, and you will be less likely to fall into them.

Family

In addition to being lured by men, a wife who is not careful can be lured away from her marriage by her own parents and family members.

I remember when I was in the process of leaving my parents, one of my family members told me that "Blood is thicker than water." Have you ever heard that saying? The Bible does not support this kind of thinking. This statement is deceptive as it relates to relationships. The Bible teaches us that when we enter into the marriage union, we are entering into a covenant relationship. This relationship is different than any other kind of relationship because it is life-long rather than temporary. Nowhere in the Scriptures are we admonished to become one flesh with our parents, siblings, aunts, uncles, etc. Our relationships with our parents and family members were meant to be broken. This is unlike our relationship with our husbands which was meant to be life-long. This fundamental truth is quickly being lost as more and more marriages are breaking up and spouses are returning back to their parents to strengthen that bond. This is opposite to the teaching of the Bible.

Wives who have not detached themselves from their family many times can be in a tug of war situation between their husbands and their families. The husband may give a direction for his wife only to find that he is undermined by her family. Family is a major reason marriages have problems. Simple things like deciding where to spend Thanksgiving and Christmas can cause schism in the marriage.

I remember seven years into my marriage wrestling as to whether or not it was right for me to leave my family. Then one day, the Lord highlighted a verse that was a real comfort to me. The verse is Psalm 45:10. After reading that verse, I wanted to make sure I understood it correctly just in case there was a chance that I was totally off base and perhaps reading too much into the Scripture. I decided to turn to theologians of the past to hear their take on the verse. Here is what Matthew Henry, a great scholar and preacher from the 1600s, had to say:

> She must renounce all others. Here is the law of her espousals: 'Forget thy own people and thy father's house,' according to the law of marriage. Retain not the affection thou hast had for them, nor covet to return to them again; banish all such remembrance (not only of thy people that were dear to thee, but of thy father's house that were dearer) as may incline thee to

look back, as Lot's wife to Sodom."[1]

To many of us today, these would seem like harsh words. Who would do such a thing? Banish all remembrance of your family? This sounds absurd. Should people really think like this? Let's fast forward a bit to a time period that's a little closer to ours. The year was 1810, and missionary Adoniram Judson was about to set out to evangelize Burma. Before his departure, however, he fell in love with Ann Hasseltine. After declaring his love for Ann, he wrote the following letter to her father:

> I have now to ask, whether you can consent to part with your daughter early next spring, to see her no more in this world; whether you can consent to her departure, and her subjection to the hardships and sufferings of missionary life; whether you can consent to her exposure to the dangers of the ocean, to the fatal influence of the southern climate of India; to every kind of want and distress; to degradation, insult, persecution, and perhaps a violent death. Can you consent to all this, for the sake of him who left his heavenly home, and died

31

for her and for you; for the sake of perishing, immortal souls; for the sake of Zion, and the glory of God? Can you consent to all this, in hope of soon meeting your daughter in the world of glory, with the crown of righteous, brightened with the acclamations of praise which shall redound to her Savior from heathens saved, through her means, from eternal woe and despair?[2]

What father would read a letter like this one and consent to such a thing? Better yet, what girl in her right mind would hear her dad read a letter like this and say, "Yep, this is the kind of life I was dreaming of." Most of us today would have a hard time with this. Unlike us, believe it or not, Ann's father told Adoniram that Ann could make up her own mind on the matter, and that she did. They were married on February 5, 1812. Ann left it all for a future full of uncertainties, but one thing was certain. Both Ann and her father had a clear understanding that this was the end of their time together.

Friends

This brings me to the issue of friends. If the wife is

not careful, friends, whether past or current, can be an issue in her marriage. Sometimes a wife might confide too much in a friend or become too dependent on her friends. Have you ever found yourself running to your best friend's home or grabbing the phone to give her a call when you and your husband get into a quarrel? A friend may be temporary anesthesia for the pain you are be experiencing. If so, you just might be training yourself to become dependent on that friend—perhaps for comfort or to side with you. Thus, a wife's friends can be a problem to her solidifying a good marriage with her husband and serve as another lure that the enemy uses against her.

Children

Another potential concern to consider is that of children. If the wife is not careful, she can be lured away from her husband by her own children.

Normally, the bond in the parent-child relationship is pretty strong. For this reason, it is easy for a wife to put her children before her husband. I remember once going to the store and having an awkward experience relating to this very subject. I was standing in line at the register waiting for a certain lady to finish checking out only to notice that while she was talking to the cashier, she kept looking back at me. I couldn't help overhearing her conversation that she was planning to leave her husband so she could put her daughter first. She seemed aggressive in her looks, so I was a little intimated by her. Why was she looking at me while talking to the cashier? Was she hoping I would join in and affirm her in her decision? I think perhaps so. I wasn't sure what to say to her, but I decided to say something. I looked at her and said, "That's not what the Bible says to do." As if I had hit her in the face with a baseball bat, my brief relationship with her ended as she left the store. It was a shaking experience for both of us.

I came to understand that the reason it was such a shaking experience was because I was being privy to a crime that was about to take place. It is just as if I overheard two men talking about going to rob the bank downtown. Would I remain silent, or would I call the police? I would call the police. Similarly, this lady was about to commit a heinous crime against her husband, and I needed to say something. There is a verse in Leviticus that teaches us this principle. Leviticus 5:1 states, "And if a soul sin, and hear the voice of swearing, and is a witness, whether he hath seen or known of it; if he do not utter it, then he shall bear his iniquity." I knew nothing about this woman other than what she said, but suppose she had grown up in a Christian home and knew right from wrong. Was the Lord using my mouth to give her a reminder to change course? Whether she grew up in a Christian home or not, marriage is an institution set up by God. No matter what a woman's background, putting your children before your husband is a bad idea.

Another example comes to mind as I met another woman who had a similar story. This lady said she left her husband because he wanted to spank her kids. Her children were from a previous marriage, and her new husband was their stepfather. I might add that this was a church going lady. This wife left the one man who wanted to show her family love. Real love will discipline. This wife missed the mark on what true love looks like.

Still yet, I met another woman at the mall who told me that she left her husband to take care of her grandchild. What in the world is happening? This is a never ending problem. Why are so many wives leaving their husbands for the sake of their children? Something is wrong with this!

Dr. Jay E. Adams, a Christian counselor, writes:

> When wives vainly attempt to fight loneliness by substituting children (especially a son) for husbands, or when husband try to do so by burying themselves in business (or busyness), they err greatly. Under God, a husband and a wife must put one another first, before all others, and all activities. Only in that way will children be free to leave home without heartache when the time comes. And, the marriage will grow. The relationship between parent and child is established through birth (or adoption); the relationship between husband and wife, by covenant promise. This contrast between the temporary parent-child relationship and the permanent husband-wife union once again forcefully points up the uniqueness of marriage in God's plan for human beings.[3]

All I can say is that the devil will give a wife any and every excuse to push her out of her marriage. It could be a career, money, her husband's health, etc. Nevertheless, God wants her to remain in her marriage, so she can be under His blessing.

Chapter 4

Reconciliation

*D*ear wife, unless you have been given a Biblical escape, I encourage you to reconcile to your husband. Don't let the devil bring you out in the open to plummet you. Go back under the umbrella where you can be protected. You see, if Satan can destroy the wife, he can destroy the home. If he can destroy the home, he can destroy the nation. If he can destroy the nation, he can destroy the world. The place of the wife and the place of the husband in the home are like two great pillars that everything is built on. Removing one out of its place results in a fractured infrastructure. God has set up the home to be the nucleus by which we can have a strong foundation in society, but if that foundation is removed, we are of all people most miserable. You see, your place as a wife is absolutely vital to the success of life—not just for yourself but your husband, your children, and even those who follow. It is, therefore, no wonder that the devil wants to eject you out of your place.

The Edwards

Have you ever heard of the lineage of the Edwards family? Perhaps you know of the famous preacher Johnathan Edwards, who preached one of the greatest sermons still remembered today, *Sinners in the Hands of an Angry God*? Well, the saying is that behind every great man is a great woman. That woman in Mr. Edwards' life was his wife, Sarah Edwards. They lived during the 1700s.

It is said that after the great evangelist George Whitfield, a single preacher, visited the Edwards home, he wrote in his diary that "He did hope that the Lord would send him as a wife such a woman as Mrs. Edwards, whom he considered the most beautiful and noble wife for a Christian minister that he had ever known. If there be a more charming tribute to woman than this, I have not seen it."[1] Besides being respected by other men, Sarah was deeply admired by her own husband. Mr. Edwards said that Sarah's spirit encouraged his spiritual life, and her presence brought him peace. He would often read to her the notes he had written earlier in the day because he valued her thoughts and responses.[2]

Sarah's influence, however, didn't just end there. In addition to being a lovely wife, Mrs. Edwards was an influential mother. She had eleven children and was primary in training them up in the values necessary for life. This resulted in the Edwards family leaving behind a notable legacy. In 1900, A. E. Winship published *Jukes-Edwards: A Study in Education and Heredity* in which he contrasted two families. One family had hundreds of descendants who were a drain on society. The other, descendants of Jonathan and Sarah Edwards. It was discovered that Jonathan and Sarah Edwards' made contributions to society that included:

- 13 college presidents
- 65 professors
- 100 lawyers and a dean of a law school
- 30 judges
- 66 physicians and a dean of a medical school

In addition, there were eighty holders of public

office including:

- three U.S. senators

- mayors of three large cities

- governors of three states

- a vice president of the U.S.

- a controller of the U.S. Treasury

- Members of the family wrote 135 books. . . . edited 18 journals and periodicals. They entered the ministry in platoons and sent one hundred missionaries overseas, as well as stocking many mission boards with lay trustees (Dodds, *Marriage to a Difficult Man*, 31-32).[3]

Speaking solely of Sarah Edwards, Mr. Winship noted,

> Much of the capacity and talent, intensity and character of the more than 1,400 of the Edwards family is due to Mrs. Edwards. None of the brothers or sisters of Jonathan Edwards had families with any such marvelous record as his, and to his wife belongs not a little of the credit.[4]

What would this picture have looked like if Sarah had abandoned ship? Pretty grim. This is not to say that Sarah was always in harmony with her husband. She once wrote:

> The next morning, I found a degree of uneasiness in my mind, at Mr. Edward's suggesting, that he thought I had failed in some measure in point of prudence, in some conversation I had with Mr. Williams Hadley, the day before. I found, it seemed to bereave me of the quietness and calm of my mind, in any respect not to have the good opinion of my husband. This, I much disliked in myself, as arguing a want of a sufficient rest in God, and felt a disposition to fight against it, and look to God for his help."[5]

But what would have happened if Sarah didn't look to God for help and instead, like so many today, argue or threaten to walk out of the marriage when their husbands do or say something that rubs them wrong? I doubt we would have ever heard of her nor possibly her husband.

Why am I sharing this with you? The decisions you

make today will not only have a lasting impact on you but also those that are influenced by you. Your decisions today will either set you up to fail or set you up to prosper. Dear wife, you have the whole host of heaven wanting you to prosper and the whole host of hell wanting you to fail. What will you choose? You cast the deciding vote. If you choose to remain in the marriage, then the next chapter will deal with how to live with a difficult husband.

Chapter 5

How to Live With a Difficult Husband

So, how do you live with a difficult husband? Perhaps Abigail's story will help.

Abigail's Story

In Abigail's story, there was a man named David. David was to be the king of Israel but was not in the office as yet. Instead, he was on the run from the King at that time whose name was Saul. Saul wanted to destroy David. While on the run, David found some herdsmen with a great host of flocks, and he and his men helped them in protecting the animals. Later on, David was hungry and contacted the man who owned all these flocks asking for some food. The man was a wealthy man but stingy and evil—not to mention that he was also a drunkard. His name was Nabal. Nabal refused to give David anything to eat, and so David girded up his sword and went with his men to kill Nabal.

Fortunately for Nabal, he had an understanding and beautiful wife. Her name was Abigail. When Abigail learned that David had evil in mind towards her husband, Abigail hurried to take David and his men some food. When she found him, she begged him to let her husband's wrong doing be on her and persuaded him not to avenge himself and commit murder. David regarded what she had done and spared her, her husband, and all that he owned.

After all this upheaval, Abigail returned home only to find Nabal drunk. She realized there was no point in telling him anything that evening, so she waited until the next morning. The next day when he was sober, she told Nabal all that had happened. The news apparently shocked him so badly that the Bible says "that his heart died within him, and he became as a stone. And it came to pass about ten days after, that the LORD smote Nabal, that he died." I encourage you to read the entire account for yourself in 1 Samuel 25. It is a fascinating story and one with a happy ending for Abigail.

what can we learn from this woman Abigail? According to the Bible, Abigail was married to a man who was:

- churlish or stingy

- evil in his dealings

- a son of the devil

- hard to talk to because he flies into a rage

- foolish

- a drunkard

On the other hand, Abigail was:

- a woman of good understanding

- beautiful

- kind and giving

- a protector of her husband

- a person who had good timing

- a person who knew the Scriptures

When looking at this couple, the lopsidedness in their marriage is obvious. They were not even close to being on the same page, yet in-spite of her husband,

Abigail handled this matter in a way that teaches us as wives how to live with a difficult man. Instead of saying, My husband is an awful man. Who cares if he dies! Rather, she hasted to help save his life. Some might argue that she was trying to spare hers also, but she told David to let her husband's sin be on her. Apparently she was willing to die for him if need be. Maybe Abigail must have known what we all say at the altar, "For better or worse, in sickness and in health," or perhaps she understood the love described in 1 Corinthians 13 "Charity suffers long, and is kind . . . seeketh not her own, is not easily provoked, thinketh no evil. . ." Just maybe Abigail remembered Leviticus 19:18 which says, "Thou shalt not avenge, nor bear any grudge against the children of thy people, but thou shalt love thy neighbour as thyself: I am the LORD." Maybe when Abigail was angry at Nabal or thought of getting him back for all the hurtful things he had done to her, she looked ahead to Romans 12:17-21,

> Recompense to no man evil for evil. Provide things honest in the sight of all men. If it be possible, as much as lieth in you, live peaceably with all men. Dearly beloved, avenge not yourselves, but rather give place unto wrath: for it is written,

Vengeance is mine; I will repay, saith the
Lord. Therefore if thine enemy hunger,
feed him; if he thirst, give him drink: for in
so doing thou shalt heap coals of fire on his
head. Be not overcome of evil, but
overcome evil with good.

Whatever the reason, Abigail's life exemplified this
verse, "She will do him good and not evil all the days
of her life" (Proverbs 31:12). This she did all the way
to the end. Abigail did not run off from her husband
—which is what many people might counsel a wife to
do in a situation like hers. After all, her own servant
told her that her husband "is such a son of Belial, that a
man cannot speak to him." Even so, Abigail held the
fort. As a result of being patient, God freed her from
that marriage.

There is an interesting verse my pastor once
pointed out in a sermon. It is taken from Isaiah 30:7
which states, "Their strength is to sit still." This is
similar to the verse "Be still, and know that I am God"
(Psalm 46:10). It is in our stillness that God will work
mighty and awesome miracles on our behalf if we
would but only put our trust in Him and live this life
His way instead of ours. It is when we look to take

matters into our own hands that we can make a mess of things. We can wind up causing ourselves great and unnecessary pain.

Peter's Counsel

Apparently, the Lord realized that many wives would have to live with difficult and even unbelieving husbands, or He would not have inspired the Apostle Peter to write the following words. Please take time to really consider these verses and the power inside them.

> Likewise, ye wives, be in subjection to your own husbands; that, if any obey not the word, they also may without the word be won by the conversation of the wives; While they behold your chaste conversation coupled with fear. Whose adorning let it not be that outward adorning of plaiting the hair, and of wearing of gold, or of putting on of apparel; But let it be the hidden man of the heart, in that which is not corruptible, even the ornament of a meek and quiet spirit, which is in the sight of God of great price. For after this manner in the old time the holy women also, who

trusted in God, adorned themselves, being in subjection unto their own husbands: Even as Sara obeyed Abraham, calling him lord: whose daughters ye are, as long as ye do well, and are not afraid with any amazement (1 Peter 3:1-6).

What is Peter saying? The Apostle Peter was not simply talking about our speech when he used the word "conversation" but rather the manner in which a wife carries herself before her husband. I think it is wonderful that the Lord cares so much for us that He would provide the answer to our tough situations. You are probably wondering if what Peter says to do really works. Well you saw it with Abigail, but let me show it to you in another woman also. She is a pastor's wife in my little city.

The Pastor's Wife

At one church I visited, I heard this awesome testimony of the pastor's conversion. I have to admit, looking at this pastor and his wife, I would have never guessed that they would have had a story like this. The pastor said that he had been a very wicked man. He talked about his indulgence in pornography and his thirst for the bottle. He said his wife was also a very heavy drinker, that is, until she started to go to church. After his wife started attending church, he soon began noticing a change in her lifestyle. For one thing, she was no longer scolding him for watching dirty movies. Instead, she would pray. One day, he came home only to find that her bottles of liquor were still full and sitting on the counter-top. These new behaviors bothered him and he wondered why she was not like him anymore. Finally, he decided to go to the church to find out what they were doing to his wife. When he got there, he was too shy to enter the building, so instead of going in, he peeked through the key hole and listened to the service. As you can imagine, the rest is history as the saying goes. This husband ended up surrendering his life to the Lord, and later went into the ministry. Why did he do this? It was because of the witness of his wife. The Bible says we overcome by the blood of the Lamb and by the word of our testimony (Revelation 12:11).

Let me say that when dealing with a difficult husband, if your husband has a life dominating sin like pornography or drunkenness, stop nagging him about the problem. The more attention you give to the sin, the more strength you will give to it. Am I saying you can't set up hedges, no! Hedges, yes. Turn off the cable. Throw away catalogs or images depicting nudity. Avoid places that might entice the sin. In other words, stop buying the beer for your husband. Yes, cut off the sources, but don't spend all your time absorbed in this work. There are only so many holes you can plug up. If a person is determined to do evil, they will find a way around your hedges. Rather, learn from the examples above and keep reading.

Overcoming

Dear wife, you must overcome. I want you to look up these eight verses below, write them here, and remember them when you are having thoughts of giving up.

1. Revelation 2:7

_____

_____

_____

_____

_____

_____

_____

_____

_____

_____

_____

_____

_____

2. Revelation 2:11

_____

_____

_____

_____

_____

_____

_____

_____

_____

_____

_____

3. Revelation 2:17

_____

_____

_____

_____

_____

_____

_____

_____

_____

_____

_____

_____

_____

4. Revelation 2:26

_____

_____

_____

_____

_____

_____

_____

_____

_____

_____

_____

_____

5. Revelation 3:5

_____

_____

_____

_____

_____

_____

_____

_____

_____

_____

_____

_____

_____

6. Revelation 3:12

_____

_____

_____

_____

_____

_____

_____

_____

_____

_____

_____

_____

7. Revelation 3:21

_____

_____

_____

_____

_____

_____

_____

_____

_____

_____

_____

_____

In addition to these verses, I want you to write

1 Peter 4:12.

_____

_____

_____

_____

_____

_____

_____

_____

_____

_____

_____

_____

_____

<u>Pray in the Spirit</u>

If you are a spirit-filled woman, make it a habit to pray daily in the Holy Ghost. Why is praying in the Spirit important? Jude says, "But ye, beloved, building up yourselves on your most holy faith, praying in the Holy Ghost" (Jude 1:20). Paul says, "He that speaketh in an unknown tongue edifieth himself" (1 Corinthians 14:4). In other words, praying in tongues will make you stronger. The Holy Ghost is given to us for our help. He wants to refresh us in His Spirit. Have you ever felt tired and worn out without having a reason to feel so? It is said that someone once asked Smith Wigglesworth, "Brother Wigglesworth, don't you ever take a vacation?"

"Everyday," he responded.

"What do you mean?"

"I pray in tongues daily and I get refreshed. That's my vacation, that's my holiday."

In addition, praying in the Spirit will make you spiritually sensitive.

> Praying in tongues helps you become aware of spiritual events and occurrences. It helps you increase your sensitivity to the workings of the Holy Spirit. People that don't pray in tongues much are not as sharp as they could be in their discerning of the moves of the Holy Spirit and the overall happenings of God.[1]

I want to encourage you dear wife to start practicing praying for at least ten minutes in tongues everyday. As a wife who is struggling in a difficult marriage, you need all the help you can get, and God wants to be the One to help you. So to recap:

Praying in the Spirit in tongues will:

- build you up

- refresh you

- make you spiritually sensitive

Thank the Lord

Next, I want to encourage you to thank the Lord for this marriage. The Lord wants to work something in it for your good if you love Him. Look up the verses below and write them down.

1 Thessalonians 5:18

_____

_____

_____

_____

_____

_____

_____

_____

_____

_____

_____

_____

Romans 8:28

_____

_____

_____

_____

_____

_____

_____

_____

_____

_____

_____

_____

Pray with the understanding also

In addition to praying in tongues, pray with your understanding. This means to pray in your normal language (i.e. English).

Pray that the Lord will grant you good understand (like Abigail) and wisdom in dealing with your husband.

Pray for your husband that the Lord will change

the circumstances in his life that will lead him to repentance. Don't pray that God will change your husband's will but his circumstances. Pray that his circumstances will change, so that he can use the free will God has given him to make the right choices. God will not stop a person from doing evil, but He may send help along the way for them to stop in their tracks and be rerouted (i.e David and Abigail 1 Sam. 25, Balaam and his donkey).

Abraham understood that a person had a free will. Do you remember what Abraham told the servant he was sending to search out a wife for his son? The servant has asked what to do if the woman was not willing to come back with him. Abraham said "And if the woman will not be willing to follow thee, then thou shalt be clear from this my oath" (Genesis 24:8). Abraham understood that a person had a free will. If a person is not willing to do something, you can't force them. You can pray, however, regarding their circumstances. For example, you can pray that God will take things or people out of his life. You can pray that he will feel a certain way. You can pray that the Lord will buffet him as He used Satan to buffet Job. One of God's strategies is to send plagues as we see in Revelation, Exodus etc. You can pray similarly. You can pray that God will sober him up.

The Praise and Worship Couple

Some years ago I visited a Jamaican church and met a wonderful couple with a harmonious testimony. This couple sang on the praise and worship team together, and they were always so well dressed. They even matched their outfits together. There was no question whom she belonged to and whom he belonged to. They were a unified couple. The husband was a happy, warm, jolly, and enthusiastic worshiper. He was not the kind to sit still in church. Well, I later learned that this couple was not always so jolly and coordinated in their relationship. Apparently, the husband used to be quite a night owl who loved to party. He frequented the night clubs and loved dancing. His wife however was a Christian, and she was not going to settle for a husband who liked to go off parting and dancing it up with other women.

You know when a person is really desperate to see a situation change they're going to be willing to do anything. So, this wife intensified her efforts, and she became more aggressive in seeing her husband delivered. This is what she did. After her husband left to go clubbing, she would go into his closet and anoint each article of his clothing with oil, and she would fast and pray for him. What do you think happened next? I don't know how long it took, but the Lord heard her fastings and prayers because one day her husband walked straight up the church aisle to the altar and surrendered his life to Jesus. Today, he is dancing in the house of the Lord. Praise God for a praying wife!

Prayer and Fasting

There are certain situations that are not going to be healed without prayer and fasting. When Jesus' disciples asked Him about a certain case where they could not cast a dumb and deaf spirit out of a boy, Jesus replied, "This kind can come forth by nothing, but by prayer and fasting" (Mark 9:29). When it is a case of a really big problem in your life, like a difficult husband, I would encourage you to get aggressive by fasting and praying.

How to Pray and Fast

1. Before you begin, repent for any sins in your life. For instance, did you, as a Christian believer, marry an unsaved man? If so, the first step will be to repent for

doing this to begin with (see 2 Corinthians 6:14). If you were an unbeliever at the time of your marriage or your husband was a professing believer, then this does not apply to you. If you need to repent, do so before you begin working on your husband's problems.

2. Take three days off from whatever you are doing and dedicate it to fasting (eating no food) and praying for your husband.

3. Tell your husband you would like to do this. Depending on your husband, he may be okay with that, or he may tell you it is of no use. He may say you don't have to do that. Regardless, you know that there is a problem, and even though he may not see it or recognize how serious it is, still tell him you want to fast and pray anyway. A woman who is desperate for something to change will behave like Hannah in the book of 1 Samuel 1. I encourage you to read her story and see her bitterness of soul. Now, if your husband does not know what fasting means, you can mention 1 Corinthians 7:5,

> Defraud ye not one the other, except it be with consent for a time, that ye may give yourselves to fasting and prayer; and come together again, that Satan tempt you not

for your incontinency.

In other words, tell him that this means abstaining from each other physically (intimate relations). Of course, fasting includes depriving oneself of food as well, but you may drink water. I would like to inject here that like praying in tongues, fasting will make your spiritual senses sharper and more in tune with the Lord, so that you can know what to pray concerning your husband and how to pray it.

However, if your husband tells you not to fast, I would encourage you to pray and fast secretly. Fast when you can, perhaps your breakfast or lunch, and pray always. "And thy Father which seeth in secret himself shall reward thee openly" (Matthew 6:4).

3. Pray over everything that relates to your husband. Pray over his clothes, his phone, his car, his computer, and whatever relates to him or the problem. Pray that the Lord will break the deception off of him, the lies, the strongholds, etc. If your husband is not opposed to you praying, let him see you praying for him. Don't do this to make a show or spectacle of yourself but to let the devil know that you are serious about him loosing your husband.

4. Communicate. If your husband is open, talk to him about his sins.

- Find out where it all started.

- Encourage (not force) him to repent of his sins.

- Encourage (not force) him to receive the Lord.

- Cast out the devil and tear down the strongholds. Speak directly to the devil. Tell him to leave and command that the strongholds be destroyed. (See Why Children Cry by Billy Prewitt)

5. Repeat these steps as you see necessary, and trust in the Lord for the deliverance.

In short, the things mentioned in this chapter are designed to help you be on the right track when dealing with a difficult husband. I hope you put them into practice, and trust the Lord for the results.

Chapter 6

1 Still Want to Leave

1 Corinthians 7:11

*L*et's say the wife still wants to leave the marriage, but she does not have the exception clause Jesus talks about nor did her husband forsake her. What does the Bible say about that? In 1 Corinthians 7:10 Paul writes, "And unto the married I command, yet not I, but the Lord, Let not the wife depart from her husband." But, in 1 Corinthians 7:11, Paul writes, "But and if she depart, let her remain unmarried, or be reconciled to her husband: and let not the husband put away his wife." Here we see that if the wife is determined to leave her husband, then the Lord will ask of her two things:

1) Let her remain unmarried, or

2) Be reconciled to her husband

Earlier, I mentioned the story of Fanny Crosby, the hymn writer, who left her marriage. Was Fanny Crosby in the wrong to do so? Well, according to Matthew Henry, it would seem so. He writes,

> Man and wife cannot separate at pleasure, nor dissolve, when they will, their matrimonial bonds and relation. They must not separate for any other cause than what Christ allows. And therefore the apostle advises that if any woman had been separated, either by a voluntary act of her own or by an act of her husband, she should continue unmarried, and seek reconciliation with her husband, that they might cohabit again.[1]

We don't know the whole story behind Fanny and Van's separation, but what we do know leads me to think that Fanny was in the wrong to separate. If Fanny had said to her husband, "I don't want to separate," then she would have been in the right if her husband left anyway, but the fact that she agreed to mutually separate puts her in the wrong. She did, however, fulfill the rest of the verse that says, "Let her remain unmarried." As far we know, Fanny Crosby never remarried, nor did she return to her husband. Instead, she spent the remaining years of her life performing charitable works and continuing in her writings. Are you able to live in this state dear wife, or are you going to one day want to be remarried? If you do want to remarry, Jesus said, "And if a woman shall put away her husband, and be married to another, she committeth adultery" (Mark 10:12).

You see, the Lord is not willing that the wife depart, nor does He want the husband to put away his wife. In other words, they can't just mutually agree to leave the marriage or else they would both be in the wrong. Unfortunately, it would seem that such was the case with Fanny and Van.

> There apparently was no overt unhappiness between them, but they were less often in each other's company. They still loved each other, according to Fanny, but gradually the relationship was downgraded, by mutual consent, from that of husband and wife to one of simply good friends. There

was no hint of infidelity, only of seeking support and companionship elsewhere.[2]

Dr. Adams observes: "It is obvious that one must cultivate companionship. A marriage lacking companionship is headed toward misery or divorce. All that jeopardizes companionship must be avoided; whatever promotes it must be cultivated."[3]

Remaining Friends

Sometimes a wife who does not have Biblical grounds to leave her marriage will leave but still tell her husband that she wants to remain friends with him. If this is you, I want to encourage you not to do this to your husband. The reason a wife might say this to her husband is because she feels guilty for leaving. She is like the man spoken of in Proverbs 20:25: "It is a snare to the man who devoureth that which is holy, and after vows to make enquiry." John Wesley says, "A snare - It brings guilt upon him. After - After a man has made vows to enquire for ways to break them." The Bible says that marriage is honorable, therefore, it should not be taken lightly and downgraded to the status of friends.

The wife who leaves and tells her husband she want to remain friends may in fact enjoy her husband's company. In reality, however, she does not want to live within the guidelines of marriage or learn how to deal with problems in a way that honors God. The wife should not put her husband in this awkward position. That's like a guy who murders your mother and then asks you out on a date. You would repulse that man. Similarly, if the wife is going to leave her husband, she should not ask him to be friends with her. The Lord wants to be the Church's husband. He is not seeking a semi-casual relationship.

I will say this to you dear wife, if you do not have Biblical grounds to leave the marriage and you decide to wait, then one of two things could happen: 1) The marriage might actually get better, or 2) If your husband is a wicked man, he will give you grounds sooner or later. With that said, the wife must not incite her husband to leave nor push him away. Instead, she must do her best to treat him right. Then, if her husband does give her Biblical grounds, then she will know that in the sight of God, she was not the one that lifted a finger to end the marriage.

Conclusion

*D*ear wife, I hope that the knowledge presented in *I'm Thinking of Leaving My Husband* has been useful to you. Marriage is wonderful when done right and can bring years of bliss, fulfillment, and security. When done wrong, however, it can bring many blisters, dissatisfaction, and distress. If you have Biblical grounds to leave your marriage and you do indeed leave, I pray that the Lord will lead and guide you as you move forward. If you do not have Biblical grounds to leave and decide to remain in your marriage, I pray that the Lord will bless you with great understanding, wisdom, and love in seeing your marriage healed. If you have read this book and are still determined to leave your marriage without Biblical grounds, may the Lord have mercy on your soul. Regardless of which of these three categories you fit into, if you desire to have further counseling, I would be happy to hear from you.

Notes

Chapter 2

   1.   F. B. Meyers, *Through the Bible Day by Day*, electronic ed. (Published in 1914; public domain), 1 Cor. 11:2-10. e-Sword 12.0.1.

Chapter 3

   1.   Matthew Henry, *Matthew Henry's Commentary on the Whole Bible*, electronic ed. (Published in 1708-1714; public domain), Psalm 45. e-Sword 12.0.1.

   2.   Anderson, Courtney. (1956). To the Golden Shore. Grand Rapids: Zondervan. In J. Piper (2012), Adoniram Judson: How Few There Are Who Die So Hard! Minneapolis, MN: Desiring God.

   3.   Jay E. Adams, *Marriage Divorce, and Remarriage in the Bible.* (Grand Rapids, MI: Zondervan, 1980), 20.

Chapter 4

   1.   "The Project Gutenberg EBook of Jukes-Edwards," https://archive.org/stream/jukesedwards15623gut/15623.txt, (accessed 9/17/20).

   2.   Roberts Liardon, *God's Generals: The Revivalists* (New Kensington, PA:Whitaker House, 2008), 146.

   3.   Noel Piper, *Sarah Edwards: Johnathan's Home and*

Haven, https://www.desiringgod.org/messages/sarah-edwards-jonathans-home-and-haven (accessed 9/17/20).

4. "The Project Gutenberg EBook of Jukes-Edwards," https://archive.org/stream/jukesedwards15623gut/15623.txt, (accessed 9/17/20).

5. *A Celebration of Women Writers,* http://digital.library.upenn.edu/women/pierrepont/conversion/conversion.html (accessed 9/17/20).

Chapter 5
    1. Roberts Liardon, *The Azusa Street Revival: When the Fire Fell* (Shippensburg, PA:Destiny Image Publishers, 2006), 220-222.

Chapter 6
    1. Matthew Henry, *Matthew Henry's Commentary on the Whole Bible*, electronic ed. (Published in 1708-1714; public domain), 1 Cor. 7:10-16. e-Sword 12.0.1.

    2. Bernard Ruffin, *Fanny Crosby: The Hymn Writer* (Uhrichsville, Oh:Barbour Publishing Inc., 1995), 140.

    3. Jay E. Adams, *Marriage Divorce, and Remarriage in the Bible* (Grand Rapids, MI: Zondervan, 1980), 20.

Appendix

Broken by Divorce
by Billy Prewitt

> *"Divorce is the closest you can come to death without actually dying."*

These words were spoken by a pastor in New York several years ago. He knew what he was talking about. He had seen throughout his years of marriage counseling the truth of his statement. The pain and suffering that divorce brings is devastating. It brings a brokenness to the very heart of men and women.

It is a well known fact that broken bones do not always heal properly. If a bone is not set properly, it will heal crooked creating a lasting problem. The same is true of divorce. If the wounds of divorce are not dealt with properly, then the problems become buried and do not heal well.

#1 God knows your pain

You have probably heard the verse from the book of Malachi that says that God hates divorce. It is true, He does hate it, but have you ever wondered why? While there may be more than one answer to that question, it may be safe to assume that He hates divorce because He knows how bad divorce will hurt everyone involved.

If you have ever been through a divorce or even been in close proximity to one, you are already painfully aware of the consequences. God made us in His image, and therefore, He has a deep affection for us. He does not want anything to hurt us. He knows the devastation that divorce causes. He knows the pain and insecurity that it brings to everyone around. He does not want any of us to suffer that kind of devastation in our lives. It only makes sense that God hates divorce.

#2 God loves divorced people

Just because the Bible teaches that God hates divorce, this does not mean that God hates divorced people. No! He loves divorced people just as much as He did before the divorce happened. If the truth were known, He is watching carefully hoping that you will turn to Him in this time of greatest trial. He has comfort and stability that can be yours for the asking. Even when you don't feel like you can talk to anyone else, He will listen patiently because He cares for you. 1 Peter 5:6-7 says, "Humble yourselves therefore under the mighty hand of God, that he may exalt you in due time: Casting all your care upon him; for he careth for you."

#3 Divorce is not a sin

Did you know that the Bible does not call divorce a sin? In fact, it readily recognizes that there can be innocent parties to divorce and even allows divorce in some situations. You may not be at fault for your divorce. If that is the case, God already knows. He is not looking to punish you for something you did not do. Even if you are at fault, God knows that too. He is still willing to receive you if you repent of the wrongs you have committed.

Many times we do not realize how ready God is to forgive us. When we are willing to repent of our sins, God is ready to listen. 1 John 1:9 says, "If we confess our sins, he is faithful and just to forgive us our sins, and to cleanse us from all unrighteousness."

#4 God wants to heal you

When Jesus spoke to the people at Nazareth, He told them that part of what He had come to do was "heal the brokenhearted." If your heart is broken by divorce, Jesus can heal it. He can restore you and rebuild you into a new and even better person than you were before.

When Jesus was on the earth, He met many people that were broken. One of those was a woman that had been married five times and was living with a new boyfriend. When He spoke to this woman, He offered her hope. He told her, "Whosoever drinketh of the water that I shall give him shall never thirst; but the water that I shall give him shall be in him a well of water springing up into everlasting life."

Maybe you could use some of the water that Jesus offers. He still has water to give, and He is willing to give it to you. Let these words of His remind you that you are still the object of His love.

"If any man thirst, let him come unto me, and drink. He that believeth on me, as the scripture hath said, out of his belly shall flow rivers of living water" (John 7:37-38).

Other Resources Available

You Can Be a Happy Wife: A Look at the Wife's Role

by Rebekah Prewitt

Jesus said, "*Verily I say unto you, There is no man that hath left house, or parents, or brethren, or wife, or children, for the kingdom of God's sake, Who shall not receive manifold more in this present time, and in the world to come life everlasting*" *(Luke 18:29-30)*. In spite of what He said, many wives miss out on enjoying the "manifold more" blessings of God because they have not learned how to have a happy life now. In *You Can Be a Happy Wife: A Look at the Wife's Role*, Rebekah candidly shares her own experiences that the Lord used to teach her of how to be a happy wife. It has worked for the author, and it can work for you too!

How to Talk to Your Child About Divorce

by Rebekah Prewitt

How to Talk to Your Child About Divorce provides a step-by-step interactive approach. You will not have to guess what to say to your child in this crisis. This book will tell you exactly where to begin, what to say, and even how to say it. It is broken down into bite-sized lessons that you can start using immediately. There isn't any lengthy reading either—just simple, practical instructions. Also, to aid in your talks with your child, *How to Talk to Your Child About Divorce* is designed with worksheet activities specifically created for children of divorced parents. Best of all, the information presented in *How to Talk to Your Child About Divorce* is Bible-centered, so you can be sure that your child is getting the right help.

Has your child asked you, "Why can't you get back together?" Maybe he or she is showing signs of anger or shutting down. You will learn how to talk to your child about:

- False Guilt,
- Why Can't You Get Back Together?,
- Anger,
- Why Can't I Live With . . . ?,
- What Happens When a Child Won't Talk,
- Communication,

and much more. The worksheets are designed with elementary children in mind, and the lessons are perfectly suitable to any age including teens.

Dealing With Suicide
by Rebekah Prewitt

What does the Bible say about suicide? Is it silent on the issue as some claim? The Biblical research presented in *Dealing With Suicide* may be surprising. You will discover that the Bible, both Old and New Testaments, has real answers to the tough questions Christians often ask. Questions like:

- Why do people commit suicide?
- Did they know what they were doing?
- What does the Bible say about mental illness?
- Where did they go?

In *Dealing With Suicide*, Rebekah Prewitt also outlines:

- How to help the suicidal
- Steps the bereaved can take in the aftermath of suicide
- False teachings to avoid

Why Children Cry
by Billy Prewitt

Have you ever wondered why children cry? Have you ever noticed that one time a child will seem totally normal and then the next time they are completely going wild? Perhaps they are kicking and screaming, or throwing things, always getting in trouble, or putting their fingers in their ears to tune you out. Do you find yourself frustrated with your child's behavior and don't know what to do? In *Why Children Cry*, Billy Prewitt draws from his experiences as a teacher and minister to candidly show the reasons why children behave the way they do, and what you can do to help them.

The Baptism in the Holy Spirit:
A Pentecostal Perspective
by Billy Prewitt

Pentecostals hold that the controversial doctrine of the baptism with the Holy Spirit subsequent to salvation with the evidence of speaking in other tongues is the fulfillment of the promise of the Father, and can be progressively traced through the dispensations to the modern church as a valid and necessary experience today that God has given to His people.

What if Calvin Was Wrong?
by Billy Prewitt

What if John Calvin was wrong about eternal security? What if the penalty of Hell still remains a reality even after conversion? It is a very dangerous thing to believe that you are safe when you really are not.

Help! I am a Teacher!
by Billy Prewitt

Whether you are a first year teacher, substitute teacher, Sunday school teacher, or veteran teacher, this book is a must have. It is fun, engaging, and loaded with stress saving and practical strategies that will help you deal with challenging situations and still maintain your authority in your classroom.

Getting Married?
Premarital Preparation Course

Trinity Bible School is very excited to host a Premarital Preparation Course by Christian Counselor Rebekah Prewitt. This course is only $15.98 per couple. The subject matter of this course is centered on Biblical principles and is a four-hour audio course (mp3 format). Pastors, counselors, parents, or any person looking to offer premarital counseling will find this course to be a useful tool in equipping couples who are in preparation for marriage.

Visit: LakeCityCounsel.com or TrinityBibleSchool.com
for more info.

LakeCityCounsel.com

Bible Based Counseling

Casting all your care upon him; for he careth for you.

1 Peter 5:7

Counseling is available for a wide range of situations including but not limited to:

Adultery	Grief
Alcohol Addiction	Identity Struggle
Anger	Jealousy
Anxiety/Worry	Marriage Counseling
Children Counseling	Pastors in Crisis
Communication	Pornography
Depression	Premarital Counseling
Divorce Recovery	Suicidal Thoughts

Phone sessions are available

Visit LakeCityCounsel.com to learn more or
schedule an appointment

TrinityBibleSchool.com

Trinity Bible School provides quality online Christian training to believers who desire to be equipped and effective in working for the Lord. Whether you are a beginner or a degreed professional, we have courses designed for you.

• Earn a Certificate of Basic Christian Studies

• Earn a Master's Degree in Theology

• Earn a Master's Degree in Christian Counseling

• Take a Marriage or Premarital study course

You can start taking classes today!

CPSIA information can be obtained
at www.ICGtesting.com
Printed in the USA
BVHW011336051120
592613BV00018B/486/J